A Journey
Through Cancer

A Pastoral Guide

John Ellwood

malcolm down

PUBLISHING

First published 2020 by Malcolm Down Publishing Ltd
www.malcolmdown.co.uk

24 23 22 21 20   7 6 5 4 3 2 1

British Library Cataloguing in Publication Data
A catalogue record for this book is available from the British Library.

ISBN 978-1-912863-56-3

Cover design by Esther Kotecha
Art direction by Sarah Grace

Printed in the UK

Contents

What Others Are Saying...

John is not only a cancer survivor, but also a loving pastor and a thoughtful teacher, and what he's written is rich with understanding both of human suffering and of God's word. It did me good to read this booklet. I was not only informed, but fed – and I strongly recommend it to all those caring for someone facing a life-limiting medical diagnosis.

Steve Jones, Senior Pastor, Oxford Community Church, Team Leader, Salt & Light Advance

With 1 in 2 people in the UK facing the likelihood of a diagnosis of cancer in their lifetime, either we, or someone known to us, will undoubtedly face this issue. John's book, written out of his personal journey will therefore have wide appeal. While written from his own deeply Christian faith perspective, its practical nature will help people of all faiths and none, and the 'pastoral pointers' at the end of each chapter are a great resource for those journeying with family and friends through this brutal disease. I warmly recommend it.

Mike Beaumont, Bible Teacher, Author and Broadcaster

Some stories are too good to be true. This is a good story because it's true, and too good not to be told. It's the story of two journeys in one. The first, John's journey with cancer – raw, vulnerable, devoid of treacly sentiment. The second, John's journey with God – tender, authentic, glorious! It's a riveting read. It's also an excellent handbook for pastors, carers and friends of others like John – full of wisdom and helpful tips.

Rick Thomas, Hospital Doctor and Pastor, Salt and Light Ministries

Introduction

Cancer is very much a disease of our times. Whilst cures for many of the killer diseases of past centuries have been discovered (for typhoid, tuberculosis, smallpox, cholera and so on), the search still goes on for lasting cures for many cancers. According to the most accurate forecast to date from Cancer Research UK, published in the *British Journal of Cancer*, 'One in two people will develop cancer at some point in their lives.'[1] That is a frightening statistic, and calls for an army of medical and pastoral workers to provide good care.

As a church leader I have had some experience in offering support for cancer patients, and as a patient myself I have been the recipient of excellent pastoral care. I have been on both sides of this cancer equation.

I remember, as a new leader of a church, trying to respond correctly to the cancer diagnosis of a young woman in our congregation and finding it a daunting experience. I really didn't know where to begin in helping her and her family, or our church family. She was a remarkable young woman, vibrant and full of faith, and to watch her

---

1. https://www.cancerresearchuk.org/about-us/cancer-news/press-release/2015-02-04-1-in-2-people-in-the-uk-will-get-cancer

and her fiancée and family endure the suffering they did was heart-breaking. With fellow members of our congregation, my wife and I did our best, and, probably, in the end, made a reasonable job of supporting them, but I always felt I was fumbling in the dark and could have asked for help sooner than I did. This booklet is intended to provide some guidance to younger pastors called to care for seriously ill members of their congregations, perhaps for the first time. It may also help close friends and family members who have never had to face the challenge of providing support to a loved one but who desperately want to offer good support. To that end, I have ended each section with some 'pastoral pointers': practical ideas to help both patient and pastor in navigating this journey, as well as more theological observations to help steer the patient towards a God-centred response.

As a newly diagnosed patient, I experienced all the normal feelings of disorientation and bewilderment. I could have felt very alone, as many patients do, but I didn't simply because I wasn't. I always had many people around me. As my 'journey' with cancer progressed, I made some unexpected discoveries. In this booklet I have referred to my own experience, not because it is typical, or is a particularly dramatic story – it is neither – but because I hope it provides some guidelines as to what a 'good' cancer journey might look like.

I am a Christian, so this booklet is written primarily for other Christians, or those comfortable living life within a Christian framework. I refer to the Bible a lot! However, if it helps others gain some understanding of what dealing with cancer can look like when done from a faith perspective and to help them in thinking through their response to the Christian faith, then it will have served a useful purpose.

King David knew what it was to 'walk through the valley of the shadow of death'. But he also knew what it was to 'fear no evil' while doing so, for 'your rod and your staff, they comfort me'. Sometimes that comfort comes directly from the Lord himself, but it can also come in the form of flesh-and-blood friends, relatives and gifted shepherds working under the oversight of the great Good Shepherd.[2]

'*The* LORD *is my shepherd, I lack nothing.*'[3] That is true for both those who suffer and those who care.

---

2. Psalm 23:4
3. Psalm 23:1

1
A Shock Diagnosis

I shall never forget receiving the news that I had a form of myeloma, a blood cancer affecting the bone marrow and immune system. In February 2011, I had a blood test for an unrelated condition which, in the end, proved a false alarm. However, somebody was smart enough to spot an irregularity in my white blood cell count and recommended an immediate visit to the haematology department of the Churchill Hospital in Oxford.

As I drove past the hospital, I was dismayed to read the sign 'Cancer and Haematology'. Cancer? Surely not, I thought.

'I am afraid so,' said the consultant soon afterwards. 'Your blood results almost certainly point to a condition called smouldering, or asymptomatic, myeloma. At the moment the myeloma is not active, but it may become so. This disease is treatable but not, at the moment, curable.'

'And if the myeloma becomes active, what is the prognosis?' I tentatively asked.

'The average life expectancy is currently about seven and a half years.' He added hopefully, 'But most patients enjoy a reasonable quality of life.'

I found my way back to the car, stunned and confused. As I drove home, I was as shocked as anybody would be. This had come completely out of the blue. It never occurred to me that I might have a form of cancer; I just thought there was a minor problem with my blood. I had anticipated a sign at the hospital indicating 'Haematology', but certainly not 'Cancer'.

However, somewhat surprisingly, I didn't experience feelings of panic. I quickly realised that in terms of prognosis, seven and a half years was a lot better than the six months or a year that some cancer patients are given. Nevertheless, all the inevitable questions reared up in my mind: How long do my wife Celia and I have together? Will I miss out on seeing my grandchildren growing up? Will I be able to keep working? Should I keep working? How will my children and parents respond? Have I somehow contributed to bringing this disease about?

When I arrived home, I remember sitting in the car for a few minutes, rehearsing how I would break the news to Celia. I would endeavour to keep the drama to a minimum, try to sound matter of fact, nothing to worry about, play it down, anything to avoid a 'scene'. I needn't have worried – she couldn't have responded better. She was very calm and simply said, 'Well, we'd better pray about this. That's what we have always done in a crisis, or when we haven't known what to do. Isn't it?' So, that's what we did. And that's what we have continued to do through the whole journey.

The next thing we did was to ring a mature couple in our church, to whom we had looked for pastoral guidance for many years. I can't remember their exact words, but the gist of their response was, 'We're really sorry to hear this news. However, rest assured, we will walk with you for however long this thing lasts. We're with you, we love you.' And they have been as good as their word.

It felt like a chapter in my life had prematurely ended. And I really had no idea about the contents of the next one.

Pastoral Pointers

- At the moment of diagnosis, the main need a patient will have is for reassurance, to know they are not alone, so resist the temptation to give advice. (It won't be clear what that should be anyway!) Instead, somehow convey the assurance that you are in this for the long haul, that they will have a friend alongside. In doing so, you are not trying to be Immanuel (one of the names of Jesus meaning 'God with us'), but you are mirroring as best you can something of Jesus' faithful long-term commitment to all his followers.

- Start to pray for them, and commit to praying for them throughout this journey. And also pray for yourself that God would show you what your promise, 'I will be with you in this', may look like in practice.

- Stay in regular contact in these early days of confusion and uncertainty.

2
Metaphors Matter!

These days, cancer receives a lot of publicity: whenever a well-known figure is diagnosed their story is told, cancer charities fundraise extensively in the media, reports on the latest breakthrough drugs are frequently published. We are probably more cancer-aware than ever before. This public interest in cancer can only help patients feel they are not alone, that great efforts are being made on their behalf. However, the challenge remains for patients to fashion a strategy for dealing with the disease day by day.

Our western culture is fond of characterising an encounter with cancer as a fight. 'John Smith battled cancer for many years.' 'Susan Jones fought bravely against breast cancer for several months, but passed away at home surrounded by her family.' This is the patient as hero, who may or may not have 'won'. While any cancer patient will tell you that there are certainly times when you have to 'fight' against pain and discomfort, against unpleasant side-effects, against anxiety and possibly depression, against feelings of anger and confusion, there is a lot more to the experience than constant combat.

I suggest a better metaphor is a journey. This recognises that, in addition to the undoubted periods of struggle – chemotherapy isn't pleasant! – there are also opportunities for considered reflection, for reordered priorities, for close ties of family and friends, for times when God seems unusually close, when the small details of life suddenly come into sharp and beautiful focus. Every long journey has its joys alongside its challenges, and it is a wise traveller who manages to appreciate the new sights and sounds in amongst the difficulties.

In addition, of course, every journey has a destination. One of the keys to a redemptive cancer 'journey' is the sense of making progress, of maintaining a sense of purpose: there is meaning to this experience. *'In ALL things God works for the good of those who love him, who have been called according to his purpose.'*[4]

What 'journey's end' will eventually look like is unknown – it may be full healing or remission, it may be a final ushering in to the presence of God. However, whatever the outcome, it need not be a journey travelled alone. Wherever possible, family, friends and pastors have a vital part to play. We must do all we can to help make this a journey with meaning and significance. It doesn't have to be a relentless slog through repeated treatment regimes or a constant mental battle.

I can't tell you how important it is not to have to travel alone. As a student, I once walked on my own from Kyle of Lochalsh in the Western Highlands in Scotland to Ullapool, about forty miles north across an inhospitable but beautiful landscape. I thought, as a rather confused twenty-one-year-old, that I might somehow 'find myself' in this wild environment. All that happened was I felt exhausted most

---

4. Romans 8:28

of the way, I was eaten by midges, I smoked too many cigarettes in an effort to drive them away, I spent long hours trudging through damp mist and I arrived in pouring rain – it was a miserable experience! A companion would certainly have helped!

The cancer journey is best done with as many companions as possible, and none more so than the patient's close family and someone with a pastor's heart. Words of wisdom and spiritual insight are always welcome, but to have trusted individuals who are prepared to drop everything and just 'be there' is even more valuable.

Pastoral Pointers

David Peach, in an article entitled '5 Christian Tips for Supporting a Friend with Cancer',[5] gives the following advice to those companions who have recently joined their friend on their journey:

1. *Educate yourself*

   Find out all you need to know, but think very carefully about what you tell the patient.

   After my diagnosis, I made a decision not to scour the internet for information, mainly because I had no way of knowing what was accurate and what was not. Instead, I asked my pastor if he wouldn't mind doing that for me and then telling me what he felt would be helpful. That way, I wasn't cutting myself off from helpful information but was being shielded from the nonsense.

---

5. https://www.whatchristianswanttoknow.com/5-christian-tips-for-supporting-a-friend-with-cancer/

2. *Be there*

Your presence is often more important than words of wisdom.

This is so important. Many visitors often feel that their main priority is to 'say the right thing'. Obviously, some words of counsel are more helpful than others. However, when I think back, I remember the simple fact that people chose to show their support and affection by visiting far more vividly than anything they said.

3. *Offer help*

Be specific sometimes. Just saying, 'If you need anything you only have to ask', doesn't always work. You could make a specific offer: 'I'm very happy to do some shopping. Let's make a list together now.'

I agree. When people said that I only had to ask for help, I was grateful but never knew quite what to ask for. Also, I didn't want to cause offence, so was tempted to think up something innocuous just to please them.

4. *Create distractions*

Sure, talk about the cancer, but also talk about normal stuff. Help the patient not be totally consumed by the cancer.

This is helpful advice. It is very easy, especially in the early stages, for the cancer to take over your thoughts. There are so many unanswered questions, which will stay so for quite a while, so being helped to focus on other things is beneficial.

5. *Say the right things*

- Here are some unhelpful things:

  ○ *Anything that puts the focus on you. 'I feel helpless, but . . .'*

- o *Anything that trivialises the situation or compares it with something else. 'You'll be fine . . . don't worry.'*

- o *Avoid observations – 'You've lost weight.' 'You look fine.'*

I have heard other myeloma patients get upset when people have commented on how well they look. They are thinking, 'Yes, but don't you realise I have a serious illness? I may look fine, but I'm certainly not.'

- *Here are some helpful things:*

  - o *'I love you.'*

  - o *'I'm praying for you.'*

  - o *'I'm thinking of you.'*

- *Let them talk if they want to. Give them 100 per cent attention, put your mobile away.*

- *Don't forget the family. Ask after them.*

All of this is very sound practical advice. Cancer can sometimes overwhelm not only the patient but also those around them. This illness is 'serious' so it must require a 'serious' response, which a supporter might not feel up to giving. Actually, simple common-sense actions are often the most effective, and bring the most peace.

3
A Theology of Sickness and Healing

Before going any further, it is worth spending a few moments considering what the Bible says about sickness and healing, and its application today.

It is clear from Scripture that God heals the sick. Death, disease, spiritual oppression are all consequences of the Fall, and Jesus came to begin the process of reversing all of them – a process that will one day be fully completed in God's new creation, where *'there will be no more death or mourning or crying or pain, for the old order of things has passed away'.*[6] This is why, instead, Jesus brought life, healing and freedom, and he wanted his disciples to learn from him and follow his example. Healing was not only a major feature of Jesus' ministry, but he expected it to be part of his disciples' ministry as well. *'The Kingdom of heaven has come near,'* he told them. *'Heal those who are ill, raise the dead, cleanse those who have leprosy, drive out demons. Freely you have received; freely give.'*[7] After Jesus' Ascension, we find that they have taken his words to heart: for example, we read of Peter

---

6. Revelation 21:4
7. Matthew 10:7-8

and John successfully healing a man crippled from birth.[8]

It is clear that a gift of healing was not restricted to the original twelve apostles, for, later on in Acts, we encounter Paul and Barnabas preaching to the accompaniment of *'miraculous signs and wonders'*.[9] In a passage about spiritual gifts, Paul declares that *'the manifestation of the Spirit is given for the common good'*. These include words of knowledge and wisdom, gifts of faith and healing, miraculous powers and prophecy. *'All these are the work of one and the same Spirit, and he distributes them to each one, just as he determines.'*[10] Healing clearly took place in the early church through the power of the Holy Spirit, as individuals obediently prayed for the sick.

And today, we are still seeing people healed. The Holy Spirit is no less active now than he was in the first century and there are numerous well-authenticated accounts of sick people being miraculously healed in our day. Many of us may have been healed of some ailment as a result of someone praying for us.

However, it is also clear from bitter experience that not everyone who has been prayed for is healed. And while some may put that down to a lack of faith on the part of pray-er or patient, or perhaps poor technique, the reality is that many have been prayed for with more than a 'mustard seed' of faith by folk who have diligently searched the Scriptures to find out what Jesus and the disciples did, but whose sickness remained. Even the great apostle Paul, who saw so many healed, had occasionally to acknowledge that his praying had not been immediately effective. For example, on one occasion, he *'left Trophimus sick in Miletus'*.[11] It is no good pretending otherwise if we

---

8. Acts 3:1-10
9. Acts 14:3, 15:12, 28:8
10. 1 Corinthians 12:7-11
11. 2 Timothy 4:20

are to move towards a satisfactory theology which embraces these twin realities: God heals today – hallelujah! – but not always.

This booklet is not a theological treatise; but, suffice it to say, that I am persuaded by the idea espoused by many modern theologians (e.g. N.T. Wright, Craig G. Bartholomew and Michael W. Goheen amongst others), that we currently live 'between the ages'. To the question, 'What time is it?' N.T. Wright answers, *'The "age to come" has been inaugurated but "this present age" still continues. We live between resurrection and resurrection, that of Jesus and that of ourselves; between the victory over death at Easter, and the final victory when Jesus "appears" again. This now/not yet tension runs right through Paul's vision of the Christian life.'*[12] Or, as Oscar Cullmann put it some years ago, *'The decisive victory was won on D-day, but V-day has not arrived yet.'*[13]

'This present age' is current but passing away, and from which, through Christ's death, we have been rescued, even though we still live in it.[14] But, through Jesus' resurrection and the coming of the Holy Spirit, 'the age to come'[15] has already broken in. We therefore live 'in the overlap', in which there is evidence of both ages. Sin and death and suffering have been dealt with at the cross, but are clearly manifest in the world in which we live, and will only be finally erased in the 'new creation'. Equally, manifestations of the power of the Spirit, inaugurated at Pentecost, are very much in evidence today: miracles – remarkable events inadequately explained by reason or science – happen. They are a foretaste of the fullness of the Kingdom that is coming.

---

12. N.T. Wright, *The Resurrection of the Son of God* (London: SPCK, 2003) p. 275
13. Oscar Cullmann, *Christ and Time: The Primitive Christian Conception of Time and History*, trans. Floyd F. Filson (London: SCM Press. 1951)
14. Galatians 1:4
15. Mark 10:30; 1 Timothy 6:19

Cancer, unfortunately, is a reality; and while it may be used as a weapon against us by Satan, it is nevertheless permitted by God (as were all the sufferings of Job) for his good purpose. We all know of cancer sufferers who have passed away; but it is equally true that some cancer sufferers recover. So far, I am one of them. While this can be partly explained by some significant advances in the development of drugs and new medical treatments, I firmly believe it is also true that God often intervenes in response to prayer and faith, as well as simply demonstrating his great grace. My experience is that, while I have received top-class medical intervention with the help of the latest drugs and procedures, I have also received the kindest of pastoral care with frequent prayers for healing alongside clear evidence of the sustaining power of the Holy Spirit. It has been life 'in the overlap', the presence and power of God in an encounter with a disease from 'this present age'.

Pastoral Pointers

- It is worth taking time to think through your theology of healing. For some, healing is simply a matter of having enough faith. While that may well lead you to pray for healing with great confidence, it may also lead to considerable disappointment and, possibly, some recrimination if, for whatever reason, the patient is not healed. Pete Greig, in his book *How to Pray*, offers a helpful perspective on unanswered prayer, drawing on Jesus' suffering in Gethsemane, commenting, *'Jesus ultimately invites me to trust in his wisdom, love and power beyond my own limited capacity to understand, praying with him the hardest and most powerful prayer of all: "not my will, but yours be done".'*[16]

16. Pete Greig, *How to Pray* (Hodder and Stoughton, 2019), p. 115

- Keep reading and feeding on stories of when God clearly *has* intervened to heal people. While we have to live with the mystery of clearly attested miracles alongside the grief of losing friends and loved ones, nevertheless we are called to *'fight the good fight'* for faith on a daily basis.[17] Elders are to anoint the sick with oil and pray for them as much today as they were expected to in the first century.[18]

---

17. 1 Timothy 6:12
18. James 5:14

4
Finding a Way Through

In his book *Choices in Healing*,[19] Michael Lerner likens cancer to a parachute jump, without a map or compass, behind enemy lines. You feel in alien territory, extremely vulnerable, but have no means of navigating your way to safety. I could identify with that. Everything had changed in an instant. The future looked uncertain; any plans I had recently made were put on hold, I had been catapulted into a foreign medical world with its own language and expectations, I felt I had suddenly lost control; in short, I was confused and bewildered and, to be honest, not a little afraid.

In October 2012, I was treated with a stem cell transplant. This involved a course of chemotherapy before harvesting a good quantity of my own stem cells. These 'clean' cells were then re-introduced back into my bone marrow. In addition, I had a vertebroplasty, whereby a form of cement was injected into three vertebrae. (One of the side effects of myeloma is that some bones, notably ribs and vertebrae, are liable to fracture.)

---

19. Quoted by Maggie Keswick Jenks in *A View from the Front Line* (2007), p. 11

While Michael Lerner's image is helpful, it omits to include the fact that each 'parachutist' lands with a 'rucksack' of life experiences. When confronted with their diagnosis and the aftermath, a patient's reaction will be determined by a wide range of factors. These include their past medical history, previous responses to crises, their support system of family and friends, childhood experiences, current physical fitness, personality, their faith perspective and so on. Some people are better equipped to deal with this experience than others, which probably helps explain why they 'travel' better.

When I look back over the last eight years, I realise that I was very fortunate in being reasonably well equipped to deal with my encounter with cancer. I come from a genetically robust family (many of my grandparents' generation lived well into their eighties or nineties and my parents are currently enjoying life in their nineties). My brother and sister and I were rarely ill as children, and were encouraged to lead an active outdoor life and to brush off the inevitable bumps and bruises which ensued. I have always remained physically active and was so when confronted with myeloma. As I have already mentioned, I have a fantastically supportive network of family and friends. I have been an active Christian since my mid-twenties, well-connected to a good local church and used to handling responsibility. I am quite an optimistic person, not least because I have not suffered any significant reverses in my life (things like financial crises, relational breakdown, bereavement, physical or psychological illness). All these factors are significant blessings and have helped me in dealing with the situation I found myself in. Not everyone is so blessed, and it is helpful if a pastor or friend takes the trouble to find out a little about a patient's medical, social and spiritual background.

My own educational background has proved relevant. I have always enjoyed literature, but have found biology and chemistry almost incomprehensible. Early in this journey, I tried my best to understand the disease. I read and re-read helpful articles, I tried to work out what white blood cells did, how my immune system operated, what the drugs were targeting. I listened carefully to other patients who had a good grasp of all this, and, of course, to the outstanding medical staff who looked after me. I did my best, but I soon got hopelessly lost in the detail. For me, getting well informed about the disease did not get me very far. For others, I could see it was incredibly helpful. Their new knowledge seemed to give them a degree of control over their circumstances; they seemed to know where they were going and what the possible outcomes were.

After quite some time, I realised I needed something that fitted my personality and interests. So instead of biology and chemistry, I turned to fiction, and made a surprising discovery in an unexpected place. The character of Bilbo Baggins in *The Hobbit*[20] by J.R.R. Tolkien perfectly fitted my experience! He was just minding his own business, going about his very ordinary life when suddenly he received an invitation to go on an adventure. He wasn't impressed: 'Adventures . . . nasty disturbing uncomfortable things! Make you late for dinner!' Anyway, he went, and got caught up in an exciting and dangerous quest for lost treasure, in the course of which he gradually changed in subtle ways. He became more confident; he realised a life preserving his home comforts is really no life at all; he became a reasonable leader when he had to; and he learnt how much he depended on his new friends to survive. His journey of adventure eventually led him home again, but he wasn't the same Bilbo who had set out months before.

---

20. J.R.R. Tolkien, *The Hobbit* (Allen and Unwin, 1937)

I found this much more helpful than chemical formulae! It helped me see the whole experience in a new light. I wasn't chasing lost treasure, but I was chasing lost health. If I submitted to the invitation to go on this journey, I may find out some important things about myself, and perhaps some much needed change might result. I might even begin to move away from the shock of diagnosis and the unpleasantness of treatment to something altogether more positive. And, as a Christian himself, I wonder if that wasn't something of Tolkien's purpose in writing the book, to persuade his readers to let go of the familiar and to embrace a life that involved a new level of trust and interdependence. Strangely, my cancer journey has helped me do that to some degree.

If it is true that Jesus is Immanuel, 'God with us', in every season, then he will have the means to provide the comfort and encouragement needed to help every patient, and it will almost certainly be different for everyone. Though friends can certainly help by their suggestions and recommendations of a film or a song or a book, in the end it is Jesus who provides the resources. I can remember my pastor bringing into hospital a DVD of *The Way* – a film about four complete strangers completing a pilgrimage to Santiago de Compostela in northern Spain. Celia and I loved it, and were inspired by the idea of a spiritual journey. In fact, in the summer of 2013, after a successful first round of treatment, we rented a cottage in the area and I walked a short section of the Camino de Santiago. As it turned out, it was a Jesus-inspired choice of film.

At first, it may indeed feel like landing in enemy territory without a map or compass, but gradually God will provide the means of us finding a way through. Because God loves each of us as one of his children, he will only give us good gifts[21] and like a father buying his children presents at Christmas, he will take the trouble to give gifts which are just right for each child. There is a tailor-made map and compass, which may take many forms, for every patient.

And for the Christian, it will almost certainly involve the Scriptures, to which we will turn in the next chapter.

Pastoral Pointers

- Take time to assess the resources the patient has in terms of medical history, personality, their faith response and so on. Understand that each patient will deal with their diagnosis and treatment differently. Some will need more help than others, so be prepared to provide the level of support that your friend needs. Some people are well-resourced and will be able to draw on that, and so may simply need someone to affirm them and encourage them forward. Others may need more assistance. This might include:
  - o Gathering a group of friends to visit regularly to read and pray together.
  - o Arranging for meals to be provided on a consistent basis.
  - o Visiting often to encourage and listen and pray.
  - o Giving updates to others via email. Some patients like to give their own updates; others, me included, prefer it if someone else takes on that responsibility, at least in the early days.
  - o It may be necessary to help regulate the number of phone calls and visits. All will be well meant, but will not necessarily

---

21. Matthew 7:11

be welcome at particularly vulnerable moments, such as just after a procedure.

- Help the patient find their 'compass'. I believe God has one for everyone – he has, after all, given us '**everything** *we need for a godly life*'.[22] There *is* a way through, but it may take time and help to begin to find it, and it may include some unusual features. (*The Hobbit* wasn't the first book which sprang to mind!) It may be a particular interest or skill (music, sport, travel, film, various hobbies); it may be a particular bias (towards science, technology, medicine, economics, the creative arts); it may be to do with their job or family; it may be linked to their spiritual gifts (teaching, prophetic, use of the gifts of the Spirit). Help your friend to dig into whatever it is that will help them.

---

22. 2 Peter 1:3

5
Cancer and the Scriptures

As any hill-walker, soldier or mountaineer will tell you, when the mist and darkness descend, you have to trust your compass implicitly. It might sometimes feel as if you are heading in the wrong direction, but it is the objective accuracy of the compass needle that will lead you to safety. Similarly, for the cancer patient who puts their trust in God's revelation through the Scriptures, they will lead him or her through the darkness and confusion.

Psalm 119 is a magnificent hymn of praise to God's written word. At the start, the psalmist declares, '*I delight in your decrees, I will not neglect your word*'[23] and he continues to expand on how he '*delights*' in God's statutes non-stop for the next hundred and sixty verses! Near the mid-point he sings:

> *How sweet are your words to my taste,*
> *sweeter than honey to my mouth!*
> *I gain understanding from your precepts;*
> *therefore I hate every wrong path.*

---

23. Psalm 119:16

Your word is a lamp for my feet
a light on my path.[24]

The Scriptures aren't bitter pills to swallow, but sweet morsels to meditate on. They give us understanding to help us avoid *'every wrong path'*, and they light the way ahead. They are potentially the map and compass that we felt we lacked when cancer came crashing into our lives.

However, the Bible is a pretty lengthy collection of books, and it may be hard to know where to start, particularly when you are feeling confused. There are plenty of websites which give lists of useful Scriptures, and these are helpful starter points. Psalm 23 is on every list, and it has helped millions of Christians through the ages as they walk through *'the valley of the shadow of death'*,[25] as we will see shortly. I have read it many times and have always drawn comfort from it – how could you not? But in addition to the 'classic' Scriptures, what also helps are Scriptures which seem to become peculiarly 'alive', which speak to our hearts at a particular moment. When Jesus was tempted by Satan, he quoted relevant Scriptures three times to combat his enemy and, of course, Satan retreated. All Scripture is 'God-breathed', but finding the right Scripture at the right moment is especially powerful.

For me, two psalms resonated particularly, Psalms 27 and 112. Other Scripture passages helped along the way, but I referred to these two time and time again. Early on, I asked God to give me Scriptures from which I could draw life. Shortly after I had found out that the smouldering myeloma had gone active and that I needed treatment, I read Psalm 27. I found it a wonderful source of comfort:

---

24. Psalm 119:103-105
25. Psalm 23:4 KJV

The LORD is my light and my salvation –
whom shall I fear?
The LORD is the stronghold of my life –
of whom shall I be afraid?[26]

That verse recognised the reality of fear, but also declared that the way to combat fear was to face in the right direction – towards the Lord – and to trust him afresh. If he was really my *'stronghold'*, my safe and secure place to run to, then it follows naturally: '. . . *of whom should I be afraid?'* So, there was a way of dealing with fear after all.

I was also struck by the final two verses:

I remain confident of this:
I will see the goodness of the LORD
in the land of the living.
Wait for the LORD;
be strong and take heart
and wait for the LORD.[27]

Really? You mean David, while besieged by a vicious enemy, was confident that he would escape and enjoy life once again? That he simply had to wait for the Lord to act? That he was able to focus on his freedom, not his present confinement? We know the end of the story, that David lived to a ripe old age. Did I dare believe that for myself? Could it be that I could embrace the same confidence? I pondered on this for several days. It seemed presumptuous in the extreme, at first, but the more I meditated on the psalm the more I began to wonder whether God was speaking to me through it. However, I wasn't sure; it still felt like wishful thinking.

26. Psalm 27:1
27. Psalm 27:13-14

A couple of weeks later, when I was in a church meeting, I noticed an old friend whom I hadn't seen for some years, come in and sit at the back just as the service began. I was glad to see him there, especially as he was known to have a prophetic gift. I didn't think any more about it until, in a lull in the singing, he began to read in a loud and emphatic voice, 'The LORD is my light and my salvation – whom shall I fear? . . .' and right on until the end of the psalm. Without any word of explanation or prayer, he sat down and the meeting continued. However, he had caught my attention! Here was Psalm 27 again, read by someone who was not a regular attender, and who probably was not aware of my situation at that time. Once again, the psalm resonated, but this time it took me beyond my uncertainty to a conviction that God wanted me to embrace *this* Scripture as God's living word to me *now*. This was his promise to me – that I would be free of fear and would enjoy 'the goodness of the LORD in the land of the living'.

Space won't allow me to catalogue all the tangible expressions of 'the goodness of the LORD' over the last few years, but suffice it to say I have enjoyed life in many new ways, including a significant house move, the arrival of more grandchildren, a revised working life, special holidays, more time for family and friends, playing a part in exciting developments in my local church. God has been as good as his word. And I am sure he will continue to be.

In their book *Joy in the Journey*, Steve and Sharol Hayner chronicle Steve's treatment for pancreatic cancer from diagnosis to his final days. It is a story of courage mingled with great joy and faith and humility. For Sharol, meditating on Psalm 23 in the company of friends was a restorative experience:

Sharol

July 30

HEALTH UPDATE: *Today is day two of the first round of the new chemo regimen. Though very tired, Steve has been up, able to eat and interact with the grandkids, who spent much of the day with us. Hopefully, now, with each day, Steve will gain strength and be ready for the second treatment next Wednesday.*

FEASTING IN THE VALLEY

We continue to be grateful for your prayers and good wishes. Every day these prayers are being answered as we experience amazing peace and courage. This can only be the work of the Holy Spirit.

Recently, I sat with friends as we studied Psalm 23. I've always separated this familiar psalm into three somewhat unrelated scenarios: first, the beautiful meadow, rich in green grass and quiet waters, an idyllic place of peace and rest, free of distraction and hardship; second, the valley of the shadow of death, where the Shepherd's rod and staff protect the sheep; and third, an abundant feast in the presence of enemies.

But at this time, I read Psalm 23 differently. I wonder if the valley of the shadow of death is also where we are treated to an abundant meal even though surrounded by enemies.

I wonder if it is in that same shadowed valley where the Shepherd offers rest in green pastures, beside still waters.

Perhaps we lack nothing, not in the idyllic destination, but in the place of darkness, pain and suffering where the Shepherd provides rest and healing.

Steve and I are discovering that we truly lack nothing and are finding peaceful rest in the valley of pancreatic cancer and chemo.

The Shepherd is so faithful.

We are grateful.[28]

That is a wonderful testimony to the power of Scripture to give perspective and faith in the dark valley of cancer. It is testimony as well to the power of friendship – the friends who prayed for them both and the friends who sat with Sharol and drew life from the Scriptures with her.

Future hope

As things turned out, despite the consistent prayers and faith of many, Steve passed into the presence of Jesus a few months later. As their book clearly shows, this was not regarded as a defeat for Steve, but rather a joy-filled journey towards a peaceful transition, surrounded by family, loved and appreciated by many.

One thing a cancer diagnosis does is to bring the patient face to face with his or her own mortality. If death doesn't come now, it will, of course, come at some time, and so highlights the necessity of facing the reality of death. Is there a life after death? What is my final destiny? Am I ready?

---

28. Steve and Sharol Hayner, *Joy in the Journey* (IVP, 2015), p. 68-69. Used by permission of InterVarsity Press, www.ivpress.com

For the Christian, there is much cause for hope. All of us have attended funerals accompanied by a reassuring address, but when we become the possible focus of such a service, theology suddenly becomes personal. At some point on the cancer journey, it may become necessary for a careful pastor to gently turn the patient's attention to the future hope that faith in Jesus Christ carries.

The Scriptures are clear. For one who has expressed faith in Christ and has received forgiveness through his work on the cross, eternal life is promised,[29] death is not the end, and certainly not the victor.[30] The apostle Peter declared that Christians have been granted a 'new birth into a living hope through the resurrection of Jesus Christ from the dead', and, more than that, 'into an inheritance that can never perish, spoil or fade . . . kept in heaven for you'.[31] We live in hope, and so we can die in hope of an imperishable inheritance.

Christ rose from the dead and is now seated at the right hand of the Father, and nothing can separate us from his love, 'neither death nor life, neither angels nor demons, neither the present nor the future . . . neither height nor depth, nor anything else in all creation'.[32] When the time comes for us to pass from life to death, the Christian can be one hundred per cent certain of Jesus' continuing, eternal love.

In 2 Corinthians 4:16 – 5:10, Paul explains that though our bodies are 'wasting away' through sickness or the ageing process, our 'momentary troubles are achieving for us an eternal glory that far outweighs them all'. Moreover, one day, in the new creation, we shall have 'an eternal house in heaven, not built by human hands' (our new resurrection bodies). If we die before Christ's return, however, we

---

29. John 3:16
30. 1 Corinthians 15:54-57
31. 1 Peter 1:3-4
32. Romans 8:35, 38-39

will not drift off into a void or soul sleep, but rather will pass directly into the presence of Jesus. Paul would *'prefer to be away from the body'*, to leave this life, because he knows that to be *'at home with the Lord'* (v. 8) is infinitely better.

John Piper succinctly summarises the immediate aftermath of death for the Christian, *'To be absent from the body will mean to be at home with the Lord; a deeper intimacy and greater at-homeness than anything we can know in this life.'*[33] One grieving mother, whose adult son had recently died, when comforted by friends saying how sorry they were to hear of her loss, responded, *'No! He is not lost. We know where he is. We have placed him into the safe arms of Jesus.'*[34] An intimate home-coming indeed!

Moreover, on Christ's return, when the 'age to come' reaches its climax, Christians can take their place in the new creation, when the new Jerusalem will descend from heaven *'as a bride beautifully dressed for her husband'* and in which *'there will be no more death or mourning or crying or pain, for the old order of things has passed away'*.[35] For sure, *'Where, O death, is your victory? Where, O death is your sting?'*[36] Our ultimate future is secure in Christ.

Whether cancer affords the patient a glimpse over the precipice followed by a welcome withdrawal, or is the means of immediately passing into God's presence, a pastor will have done his or her friend a great service by helping them understand what death

---

33. John Piper, https://www.desiringgod.org/messages/what-happens-when-you-die-at-home-with-the-lord

34. Quoted in David Oliver, *All About Heaven* (MD Publishing, 2019), pp 23-24. This is an excellent examination of the nature of heaven and assurance for the Christian of what happens after death. Visit www.davidoliverbooks.com

35. Revelation 21:1-5

36. 1 Corinthians 15:55

means for a follower of Jesus, that it is not the end, but rather a glorious new beginning.

Pastoral Pointers

- Encourage the patient to see the Bible as the *'living'* Word of God. It is creative, active and dynamic (Psalm 33:6, Isaiah 55:9-11, 2 Timothy 3:16). Therefore, it can dramatically change perspectives and impart hope and faith. Encourage them to trust God to give them Scriptures to stand on and ask God to show you passages to pass on to them.

- It may be helpful occasionally, especially in moments of difficulty, to gently remind them of what God has previously said to them through the Scriptures. It is not always easy to hang on to the promises of God in tough times.

- If it becomes clear that the patient may not recover, it may be necessary to lead him or her through the Scriptures that point towards our future with Jesus. (For example, 1 Corinthians 15:50-57; 1 Peter 1:3-5; Romans 8:33-39; 2 Corinthians 4:16 – 5:10; Revelation 21:1-5).

6
On Hearing Bad News

A cancer journey takes you over undulating territory. I have heard other myeloma patients describe it as a roller-coaster ride. When a treatment regime seems to be working, when a set of blood results are positive, when you can take a holiday during a period of remission, then the sun shines and all is well in the world. However, the reverse can also happen. Another set of blood results suggests the disease is returning, a new regime of chemotherapy begins, fatigue and nausea return, and the future again looks uncertain: the storm clouds are gathering and anxiety hovers once more.

In May 2015, I relapsed and found myself back on a course of chemotherapy. This lasted six months followed by a brief six-week remission, before another relapse and another six months of chemo. During this time I was working part-time, and, on the whole managing fairly well. Psalm 27 was keeping me going! *'I remain confident of this: I will see the goodness of the LORD in the land of the living.'* Family and friends played their part. My children and grandchildren were a delight. Celia once again 'dug in', accepted the situation, put up with my negative reactions to some of the medication, faithfully ferried me to and from the Churchill Hospital twice a week: she was certainly true to her marriage vows, 'in sickness and in health'. And our pastors were still around, giving encouragement, meals, prayer and friendship. The promise they had made four years previously still held good.

As Christians, we are not immune from 'bad news'. Jesus promised that trouble will come. *'But take heart! I have overcome the world.'*[37] Jesus wins! In him, we have all we need to prevail, whatever the circumstances and whatever the outcome.

In my Bible, alongside the title to Psalm 112, I have written three dates: I assume this psalm must have particularly spoken to me on those days. On 6th February 2011, I had just received the diagnosis of smouldering myeloma. On 5th November 2014, I had just heard that there were indications in a set of blood results that the myeloma may be returning. On 16th August 2017, I was enjoying my second main period of remission.

This psalm speaks of the benefits awaiting *'those who fear the Lord, who find great delight in his commands'*.[38] These people are described as 'righteous'. None of us can claim a righteousness outside of Christ, but because we are now 'in Christ', we have been given a *'gift of righteousness'* which enables us to *'reign in life through the one man, Jesus Christ'*.[39] Now, I am well aware of my weaknesses and I have learnt more from my failures than from my few successes. I have had to repent many times. However, in my own way, I do *'fear the Lord'* and I do *'find great delight in his commands'*, no matter how incompletely I manage to obey them. And, *'in Christ'* I have a righteousness not my own, imputed to me through Jesus' sacrificial death.

---

37. John 16:33
38. Psalm 112:1
39. Romans 5:17

On that basis, I began to apprehend the marvellous promises contained in these verses. They include: that his children would be influential; that he or she would have more than sufficient to live on; that *even in darkness light dawns*; that *they will have no fear of bad news*; *in the end they will look in triumph on their foes*.[40] By grace, these are benefits the man or woman 'made righteous' through Jesus' death can surely lay hold of. This psalm doesn't shield the believer from bad news, but it does draw the sting. There is no need to fear; his heart can stay secure; and, best of all, there will come a day when we will see our enemy defeated. For the one healed, that is cancer itself overcome. For the one for whom cancer is the means into the Father's arms, it is the prelude to that glorious day when Christ returns, *the dead will be raised imperishable* and the saying, *Death has been swallowed up in victory* will come true.[41]

Bad news will occasionally come, but it isn't necessarily the end of the story. When it comes, a friend or pastor can be so helpful in standing beside a patient and assuring them that, as a believer and a reader of Scripture, fear can be banished, and ultimate victory can be theirs. Help them to cling to the promises of Scripture. They will indeed prove *sweeter than honey*!

In November 2016, I had a donor stem cell transplant, with my brother as the donor. Remarkably, both my brother and sister were a match, so I could have had two bites of the cherry if necessary! I believe the odds of this are about 16:1, so this seemed like another token of God's favour. While this procedure carried some risk (about 20 per cent of patients do not survive), another 20 per cent of patients obtain a good result. 5:1 seemed good odds to me for a favourable outcome, and by now I was confident enough to accept the risk.

---

40. Psalm 112:4, 7, 8
41. 1 Corinthians 15:50-57

God's promises through his Scriptures had proved themselves so far: why would they not continue to do so?

Pastoral Pointer

- My point is simple. Do all you can to help your friend read the Scriptures regularly, and to believe God to speak to them as clearly as God spoke to Abraham all those years ago. Paul assures us that when Abraham believed God, it *was credited to him as righteousness*.[42] This righteousness *comes by faith* and since Abraham *is the father of us all*[43] our faith in God's promises will also be credited *to us* as righteousness as well, therefore signifying God's favour.

It is not your job as a pastor or friend to keep feeding a patient God's word, though you may be used to bring his word occasionally. Through his Holy Spirit, God will speak sovereignly. It may be through you, but it is just as likely to be directly in some way, or through someone else.

This is important because the journey is the patient's; others simply walk alongside. You cannot travel someone else's journey for them. In the end, we all have to find God's resources for ourselves, or at least recognise them when provided by another. At three in the morning, even with your beloved beside you, you are all alone in the dark. And, of course, at that vulnerable time, your worst fears can rear up, menacing and very real. The mind can play its tricks, and we have an enemy who is delighted when it does, when reality and fantasy co-mingle, when the

---

42. Romans 4:9
43. Romans 4:16

peace we thought we had suddenly seems fragile in the face of a frightening array of possibilities, when the darkness of the room mirrors the bleakness of our thoughts. It is at moments like these when the Scriptures help so much, when the man or woman, who has genuinely made them their delight in more peaceful times, can choose to access their memory bank of favourite verses and speak them out in the dark and, following Jesus' example, send Satan packing.

> *They will have no fear of bad news;*
> *their hearts are steadfast, trusting in the Lord.*[44]

---

44. Psalm 112:7

7
Looking Ahead

For all cancer patients, their earthly future is uncertain. That is true for everyone, of course; but, once you have had a cancer diagnosis, it is difficult not to think ahead without wondering how cancer will impact on the days ahead. Even while in remission, there is the nagging thought that it could make an unwelcome return at any moment. Despite the Christian's assurance regarding their future hope, they are not immune from such anxiety.

One natural concern is the degree to which a patient should plan ahead. If I may not survive for long, why think in the long-term at all? It is easy, and probably prudent, to think of wills and powers of attorney, and other aspects of 'setting my affairs in order'. On the other hand, to do so brings with it a sense that all this might be needed sooner rather than later, when I would much rather look forward to many years ahead. It's a question of balance and the personality of the individual. Common sense probably dictates that it is worth sorting out a will, arranging for power of attorney in the event of incapacity, and making sure your spouse and wider family are provided for. But, an element of faith might dictate that, having done so, it's best not to think much about it thereafter.

Forward momentum is vital for those suffering from cancer. Like any journey, there will be moments of swift progress and others of tiresome delay; but any traveller needs to know that their destination is closer now than it was a short time ago. Otherwise, the exercise becomes wearisome and frustrating. The cancer journey will have times of exasperating diversion or delay. However, for it to have meaning and purpose, then the patient needs a sense of moving forward. This may be towards recovery or it may be towards a deeper spirituality and closeness with God the Father, Son and Holy Spirit or towards developing relationships with those around.

When I came home from hospital following my donor transplant, I was not allowed to attend even small gatherings for fear of infection. In effect, I now had an immature immune system which needed time to develop. I was in limbo, waiting to learn if the procedure had been successful. It was a pause in the journey, a time when I didn't seem to be moving forward. For all I knew, my brother's stem cells might be rejected, and I would then be facing a very uncertain future. I couldn't attend church, or visit the cinema or supermarket or a sports event, or even have a meal in a pub; I was stuck in the doldrums waiting for a breeze to fill my sails again. And I don't wait well! Which was probably partly why God gave me Psalm 27, which ends, 'Wait for the LORD; be strong and take heart and wait for the LORD.'[45]

However, one of my memories of those months is of new people who knew of my situation dropping by to visit, or sending a text or email. Becalmed, I nevertheless had the opportunity to spend some time with people willing to give of their time. Their love and care was much appreciated.

---

45. Psalm 27:14

It gradually became apparent through the spring of 2017, that the donor transplant had been successful, so we began to look ahead with fresh faith. We had been wondering for a while whether we should move house to be nearer to the church we were a part of a few miles up the road, as well as feeling that perhaps this was a good time for a change of location after twenty-five years in the same house. However, was this really sensible in the context of an uncertain future? Also, we were by now both in our mid-sixties, and I had just retired after nearly forty years in education. Wouldn't it just be easier to stay put? After all, if the myeloma returned, we would be on familiar ground. Sorting out the house and getting it ready to sell would take time and resources.

Or, more pertinently, wasn't this just the moment for a fresh start?

In the end, we opted for the latter option. It has proved an excellent choice for a whole host of reasons; but the initial benefit was that it gave us a clear focus for the next few months. A breeze had picked up and our months of being becalmed were over, we were moving forward again. The future suddenly seemed full of possibilities.

However, for some, it may seem that tangible progress is hard to detect. It may be that they are in the middle of a lengthy period of treatment, or a new treatment regime has just begun. Remission may seem a long way off. Finding meaning in these times is hard. Steve Hayner was severely restricted and confronted with a most uncertain future. However, he still managed to sense what God was calling him to day by day:

> *I truly don't know what God has planned. None of us really knows what the physical symptoms of my cancer will be over time. I could receive 'healing' through whatever means, or I could continue to deteriorate. Of*

course, what we would love to see is significant healing. With God, nothing is impossible, and I would certainly welcome a miraculous intervention.

But life is about a lot more than physical health. It is measured by a lot more than medical tests and vital signs.

More important than the more particular aspects of God's work in us (in the physical, social, psychological, spiritual, mental realms of life) is God's overall presence with us, nourishing, equipping, transforming, empowering and sustaining us for whatever might be God's call to us today.

Today, my call might be to learn something new about rest.

Today, my call might be to encourage another person in some very tangible way.

Today, my call might be to learn something new about patience, endurance and identification with those who suffer.

Today, my call might be to mull through a new insight about God's truth or character.[46]

Whether in remission or moving towards journey's end, the patient needs to perceive meaning in the experience. He or she may be able to find significance on their own or they may need some help.

On a more mundane note, I found I needed marker points along the way. The house move gave an immediate focus, but what about

---

46. *Joy in the Journey*, p. 61-62

beyond that? Celia and I have found that the simple practice of having things to look forward to is immensely stimulating. That is probably true for everyone, but it has an added significance if you have a serious illness. It might sound counter-intuitive, but we have found the best response to an uncertain long-term future is to plan for a certain mid-term future. Book a visit to the theatre with friends, book a family holiday, take your place on the welcome team or children's work or preaching rota at church, keep regular weekly appointments. They are all a way of rejecting uncertainty and replacing it with definite to-be-looked-forward-to moments and activities. The 'land of the living' is a good land and to be enjoyed!

Pastoral Pointers

- Try to assess whether the patient feels as if they are making progress in some way or whether they feel 'stuck' or, in some way, 'becalmed'.

- They may need some encouragement to see the progress they have made in recent weeks, perhaps in terms of their character or in perceiving what God has been doing in their lives.

- It may be that, in these moments, to simply pray that they may know the reality of God's presence is important. Steve Hayner's words are pertinent, '*More important than the more particular aspects of God's work in us . . . is God's overall presence with us nourishing, equipping, transforming, empowering and sustaining us for whatever might be God's call to us today.*'

8
Lessons Learned

Teach me your way, LORD;
lead me in a straight path
because of my oppressors.[47]

It was good for me to be afflicted
so that I might learn your decrees.[48]

Both these extracts from the Psalms suggest that 'oppressors' and 'afflictions' can be amongst our best tutors. John Piper wrote a little booklet called *Don't Waste Your Cancer*. As the title suggests, he urges his readers to learn the lessons an encounter with cancer brings, and to use it as an opportunity to glorify God.

Piper suggests eleven ways in which we can 'waste' our cancer by failing to understand the purposes God may have in mind as we walk this journey with him. There is purpose in this encounter and much to be learned, from practical life lessons to the process of being drawn into a deeper relationship with Jesus. Piper declares,

---

47. Psalm 27:11
48. Psalm 119:71

We waste our cancer if we think 'beating' cancer means staying alive rather than cherishing Christ. Satan's and God's designs in our cancer are not the same. Satan designs to destroy our love for Christ. God designs to deepen our love for Christ. Cancer does not win if we die. It wins if we fail to cherish Christ. God's design is to wean us off the breast of the world and feast us on the sufficiency of Christ. It is meant to help us say and feel, 'I count everything as loss because of the surpassing worth of knowing Christ Jesus my Lord' (Philippians 3:8) and to know that therefore, 'to live is Christ, and to die is gain'(Philippians 1:21).[49]

This is a timely reminder to learn from the apostle Paul and seek to embrace all that life throws at us as an opportunity to turn our hearts and minds towards Jesus and seek to know him in a new and deeper way. For many of us that is certainly a different way of viewing cancer – as an instrument in God's hand to help us know Christ more. To begin to assent to the psalmist's conclusion that *'it was'* (past tense) *'good for me to be afflicted, that I might learn your decrees'*. Perhaps, after the events of his 'affliction', when he had time to recover and process his experience, he had come to see the good hand of the Lord in his suffering. After my second relapse had ended, I gave some time to reflecting on the previous few years, and seeking to identify the lessons I had been given the opportunity to embrace.

Bilbo Baggins returned home after his adventure, the same but different. His physical appearance hadn't changed and he still loved his little Hobbit hole, but he also knew that home comforts would no longer satisfy, and that relationships and joint ventures mattered.

49. John Piper, *Don't Waste Your Cancer* (Crossway, 2011), p. 10

Adversity faced with others had changed his view of the world.

Here are a few of the lessons that I hope I have personally learned on this journey. None of these are particularly remarkable or unusual, some might feel rather clichéd, but they are life lessons nonetheless.

Treasure the moment

Steve Hayner mentions a poem by E.E. Cummings which resonated with him. It begins:

> *i thank You God for most this amazing*
> *day: for the leaping greenly spirits of trees*
> *and a blue true dream of sky; and for everything*
> *which is natural which is infinite which is yes . . .*[50]

During treatment, he found these lines mirrored his heightened awareness of the beauty of the natural world. We may have read of seriously ill patients suddenly becoming aware of birdsong or spotting the first signs of spring on a branch outside their window. It seems that details which we previously ignored or barely noticed, suddenly come into focus when we find ourselves set to one side. Gerard Manley Hopkins expresses in words what a skilled photographer would capture today on film, in the opening lines of 'Pied Beauty':

> *Glory be to God for dappled things –*
> *For skies of couple-colour as a brinded cow;*
> *For rose-moles all in stipple upon trout that swim;*

---

50. E.E. Cummings, 'i thank You God for this most amazing' (New York: Oxford University Press, 1950)

Fresh-firecoal chestnut-falls; finches' wings;
Landscape plotted and pieced – fold, fallow and
plough . . .[51]

Both poets give thanks to the Creator for the intricate details in his created works. In recent years, I have found myself stopping and observing the natural world with more care than before. I have also bought a good camera and attempted to master the art of recording natural detail. There is a long way to go, but I have at least started, and take great pleasure from doing so. I once even managed to photograph a kingfisher!

It is about learning to slow down, to treasure the moment, to take time to notice not only my surroundings, but to pay closer attention in a conversation or take note of the expression in the face of the person I am talking to. The big picture matters, but so do all the small details.

Giving thanks

Paul's injunction to *'give thanks in all circumstances'* is always challenging in unpromising situations. However, he consistently recommends this[52] because he knows that there are causes for gratitude and contentment in every circumstance.[53] It is just a question of identifying them in amongst the difficulties! I have found that gratitude helps protect me from the bitterness and resentment which could so easily spring up in the wake of a particularly gruelling stage in the journey, and focus instead on the sometimes small or hidden blessings.

---

51. Gerard Manley Hopkins, 'Pied Beauty' (1877).
52. Ephesians 5:20; Colossians 3:17; Hebrews 13:15
53. Philippians 4:11-12

In particular, I am thankful for the people in the circumstances. For my pastors for their unstinting support in prayer, visits, meals and counsel, for being there throughout. For my children, in the maturity they have shown in dealing with this in their own way. For friends, in praying and visiting. And, of course, for Celia for being all a patient wife can be. Thank you!

The value of rest

I have always been prone to busyness and, at times, overwork, probably rooted in a misplaced search for significance. I might have known, as a younger man, the theory of locating my value in my identity as a child of God. However, in practice, I found as much, if not more, value in activity – 'I am what I do'. As teachers well know, there is always more that can be done, and often I didn't know where to draw the line. When your employment is suddenly interrupted, whether by illness or unemployment, questions of value, status and significance emerge. If I am not identified by what I do, where does my true identity reside?

This period of forced unemployment meant I had to address this question. I had the choice of resenting the interruption, or embracing the truths found in Ephesians 1 – that, before anything else, I am chosen, I am an adopted child of God, I am redeemed, I am *'included in Christ'*,[54] and I am *'marked in him with a seal, the promised Holy Spirit'*.[55] All that was more important than being a headteacher or church leader. This turned out to be a journey within a journey, of fully accepting who I am *'in Christ'*, of gaining a fleeting glimpse of

---

54. Ephesians 1:13
55. Ephesians 1:13

what Paul might have meant in declaring that the consuming passion of his life was *'the surpassing worth of knowing Christ Jesus my Lord'*.[56]

The good thing about enforced unemployment is that it is also enforced rest! With hindsight, I can now see that, in 2012, for a variety of reasons, I needed a period of rest. Somewhat tongue in cheek, the Scottish author and minister George Macdonald (1824-1905), once said, *'Work is not always required of a man. There is such a thing as sacred idleness, the cultivation of which is now fearfully neglected.'*[57]

I had my period of idleness, some of which I trust had its sacred moments with plenty of opportunity to read and meditate on what God might be doing in this season.

Reordering priorities

In the period away from work, I also had the opportunity to reassess my priorities and address the question of what was really important in life. Like most people in this situation, I came to the conclusion that relationships should come top, way beyond work. Somebody once quipped, *'Nobody on their deathbed ever said, "I wish I had spent more time in the office."'*[58] How true! However, there are probably many who regretted not spending enough time with their family and friends. Now was an opportunity to ensure I would never say that. In the end, I decided to step down to a part-time role in the school that I worked in – a decision I never regretted, for it released time to develop relationships and interests. It wasn't the whole reason, but my interaction with cancer was certainly very much part of it.

---

56. Philippians 3:8
57. George Macdonald, published May 1907
58. See https://www.cs.cmu.edu/~roni/quotes.html. Attributed to Senator Paul Tongas

Plan ahead

One word which crops up frequently in conversations about cancer is 'uncertainty'. None of us know the future, but cancer sufferers especially so. Past assumptions about achieving our 'threescore years and ten' and more, vanish overnight. Our earthly future can look brief and bleak and full of unknowns.

To counteract this lack of clarity, Celia and I quickly found it helpful to plan short and mid-term 'treats' to look forward to. I had forgotten how much, as a child, I had looked forward to Christmas, birthdays and school holidays. They helped deal with periods of boredom or of missing home. Now, when I felt well enough, we planned short stays in the West Country and the Lake District, and two foreign holidays in Spain and Italy, as well as occasional trips to visit one of our sons in Brussels. They were beacons on the horizon to look forward to, providing stubborn points of certainty in the face of an unknown and sometimes frightening future.

The power of the Scriptures

While I knew that the Scriptures were powerful before I fell ill, I am now more convinced than ever.

> *For in the day of trouble*
> *he will keep me safe in his dwelling . . .*[59]

---

59. Psalm 27:5

By his grace, I have been kept safe. A few weeks ago, I had a check-up. The consultant looked at my blood results and said, 'I have rarely seen a better set of results. Looking at these, you would never know you had had myeloma.'

That sounds like the goodness of God! Some myeloma patients get a positive result from treatment, but at the moment we are very much in the minority. I feel I have been strangely protected through this whole experience, and all I can do is say, 'Thank you, Lord!'

The power of prayer

Many people have prayed for me. Some prayers have been very specific, for healing; others for successful medical treatment. Am I better because of the treatment I received or because God has healed me? Good question! Since I have been the subject of many prayers and the recipient of good medical care, and am better, then I guess it must be some combination of both. Perhaps God has used the medical interventions to bring healing. It is a mystery, but I do know that when Jesus said, *'If you believe, you will receive whatever you ask for in prayer'*,[60] he was encouraging us to keep praying and to expect good answers. Prayer works!

These are some of the lessons I have learnt on the journey. I dare say I might have learnt them anyway at some point, by some other means, as they are hardly earth-shattering revelations, but I might have had to wait a few more years. If it is true that *'in all things God works for the good of those who love him, who have been called according to his purpose'*,[61] then my interaction with cancer has served as an effective tutor.

---

60. Matthew 21:22
61. Romans 8:28

Pastoral Pointers

- At some point, ask the patient what they have so far learnt through their cancer journey. If they initially say, 'Nothing really', perhaps start the ball rolling by telling them what you have observed in caring for them. Maybe, suggest that they write a few things down. It is immensely encouraging to see on paper areas in life where there has been growth. It gives meaning to the periods of uphill struggle.

- The pastor or friend may also be able to gently ask the patient what unforeseen benefits he or she can see in the experience. This might be in their character, in the way they have handled this period in their life; it may be in the way they have been able to use their time; it may be in the development of relationships; it may be in the new experiences they have had or the places they have visited. Out of this may come a renewed desire to express gratitude for God's goodness in a time of trial.

- If the patient lacks the energy or desire to plan ahead, it may be appropriate to help them plan some short or mid-term 'treats' to look forward to.

- Keep praying!

9
The 'Goodness of the Lord in the Land of the Living'

The last eight years have been amongst the most significant in my life. They have, by no means, been wasted years. They have not been without their challenges and, in terms of my working life, they turned out to herald the end of paid employment, at least for the time being.

However, in terms of finding out what it means to live 'in the overlap', it has been illuminating. Going through treatment for cancer is to experience something of the pain of 'this present age'. Illness and the threat of an early departure confronts you with your own mortality, the finite nature of our time on earth, our essential fragility and vulnerability. However, to experience two periods of full remission, to know what it feels like to enjoy good health in immediate counterpoint to ill health, to experience the love of family and friends, to know what it is to be well pastored through sickness, to enjoy some special moments while at rest, to hear the voice of God through his word, to learn something afresh about my true identity 'in Christ', is to get a foretaste of the coming fulfilment of the Kingdom, of a glorious day yet to arrive.

To summarise, it may help to keep the following at the forefront of your thinking, as you seek to care well for patients and friends:

- Companionship trumps all! Advice will be sought and good counsel will, hopefully, come to mind when it is needed, but 'presence', yours and the Lord's, matters most.

- Every patient's journey is unique, but there is assuredly a customised compass to help him or her navigate. The Scriptures are indeed a *'lamp for my feet, a light on my path'*. There IS a way through.

- This need not be a journey to no purpose. Do all you can to help your friend discern where God is in this experience – he will, bit by bit, reveal his will and his plans, as well as lessons to be learnt.

- Prayer works. Jesus commands it, the Holy Spirit guides, the Father responds.

- This can be life 'in the overlap' – pain and difficulty for sure, but the chance to experience *'the goodness of the Lᴏʀᴅ in the land of the living'* alongside little foretastes of coming glory. Cancer affords a glimpse into the future: today's 'land' lived with Christ is good, but there is a better 'city' yet to dwell in.

If you have read this as a pastor looking after a member of your congregation, or a faithful friend, or a loving family member, I pray you may be able to travel redemptively as a good companion, to help them find meaning during their treatment, to help them find a map and compass to lead them to a safe place.

> *Surely your goodness and love will follow me all the days of my life, and I will dwell in the house of the Lᴏʀᴅ forever.*[62]

---

62. Psalm 23:6